Implementing the Microsoft Dynamics GP Web Client

Second Edition

Ian Grieve

Published by azurecurve Publishing

Notice of Rights

Notice of Liability

Trademark Notice

First published: April 2020

ISBN 978-0-9930556-7-6

https://publishing.azurecurve.co.uk

About the Author

Ian Grieve is the Lead ERP Consultant at ISC Software Solutions Ltd., a Microsoft Partner, VAR and ISV headquartered in the United Kingdom of Great Britain & Northern Ireland and with an office in the Republic of Ireland. He is an Advanced Credentialed Professional in Microsoft Dynamics GP by the Association of Dynamics Professionals and was a Microsoft® Most Valuable Professional for Microsoft Dynamics GP between 2013 and 2018.

Ian has worked with Microsoft Dynamics GP since 2003 and, over the years since then, has dealt with all aspects of the product life-cycle from presales, to implementation, to technical and functional training, to post go-live support and subsequent upgrades and process reviews.

Ian is the author of *Microsoft Dynamics GP 2013 Financial Management*, *Microsoft Dynamics GP Workflow (first, second and third editions)* and *Implementing the Microsoft Dynamics GP Web Client,* co-author of *Microsoft Dynamics GP 2013 Cookbook* and *Microsoft Dynamics GP 2016 Cookbook*, produced the *Microsoft Dynamics GP Techniques* online learning course and was the technical reviewer for several Microsoft Dynamics CRM books published by Packt Publishing.

In his spare time, Ian runs the *azurecurve|Ramblings of a Dynamics GP Consultant* (http://www.azurecurve.co.uk) blog dedicated to Microsoft Dynamics GP and related products. In 2017 he launched the *azurecurve|Microsoft Dynamics GP Table Reference* website (http://gptables.azurecurve.co.uk).

Acknowledgement

Thanks to my parents for their support through the years and my employer, ISC Software, for giving me the opportunity to work with clients in many different fields and, not least, for being open to me taking on outside projects such as this book.

I also owe thanks to all of the clients I have worked with over the years, whose needs and questions have prompted me to learn ever more about Microsoft Dynamics GP, thereby putting me in a position to write this book.

Table of Contents

Preface

Microsoft Dynamics GP is a popular enterprise resource planning (ERP) application used by tens of thousands of sites around the world to keep the accounting, financial, distribution and manufacturing functions running day in and day out.

Microsoft Dynamics GP has traditionally been accessed via client software installed directly on the user's computer, as a published application or remote desktop to a terminal server. A few years ago the Web Client for Microsoft Dynamics GP was introduced.

Originally the web client used Silverlight and was supported with a limited number of browsers, but as of Microsoft Dynamics GP 2016 has been redeveloped into fully-responsive HTML5 meaning it can now be accessed using any browser and on any form factor device, from desktop PCs to notebooks to tablets and to cell phones.

Microsoft Dynamics GP in the web client can be provided in a number of ways including self-hosted, partner-hosted or cloud-hosted.

Who This Book Is For

This book is aimed at Dynamics GP users, partners and consultants who intend to implement the web client for Microsoft Dynamics GP for a single tenant. Much of the process for installing a multi-tenant deployment is the same as for a single-customer one, but is not covered in this book.

This book assumes you have a knowledge of Windows Server, Active Directory for creating users and groups, IIS and application deployments. A basic knowledge of Microsoft Dynamics GP is also required.

What This Book Covers

This book covers to of the three types of web client deployment: the single machine and scale-out deployments of Microsoft Dynamics GP.

The implementation is covered from planning to the installation of prerequisites through the installation and configuration of a scale-out deployment of the Microsoft Dynamics GP web client to logging in.

How This Book Is Structured

Chapter 1, Introduction to the Microsoft Dynamics GP Web Client, covers the basics of the web client including a look at the pros and cons of the web client versus the classic desktop client and the deployment methods available.

Chapter 2, Prerequisites of the Microsoft Dynamics GP Web Client, covers the prerequisites for installing or upgrading the Microsoft Dynamics GP web client.

Chapter 3, Microsoft Dynamics GP Web Client Single-Machine Deployment, covers the single-machine deployment implementation of the Microsoft Dynamics GP web client.

Chapter 4, Microsoft Dynamics GP Web Client Scale-Out Deployment, covers the scale-out deployment implementation of the Microsoft Dynamics GP web client.

Chapter 5, Using the Microsoft Dynamics GP Web Client, covers the process of logging into the web client, the navigation differences between the desktop and web client versions of Microsoft Dynamics GP and then how the web client can be managed.

What You Need For This Book

You will require the following for this book:

- One Windows Server 2019 with a domain controller.

- One Windows Server 2019 with Microsoft SQL Server 2019.

- One Windows Server 2019 with IIS.

- One, or more, servers with Windows Server 2019 with Microsoft Dynamics GP October 2019 Release; in the case of a single-machine deployment, this would be the same server as the one with IIS.

- The Fabrikam, Inc. sample company deployed or a copy of the live company.

Windows Server 2016 and SQL Server 2014 or 2016 are acceptable replacements for Windows Server 2019 and SQL Server 2019 listed above as both are fully compatible with Microsoft Dynamics GP.

I would recommend a trial implementation of the Microsoft Dynamics GP Web Client on a standalone test environment before implementing on a live system.

Conventions

To help you get the most from this book and keep track of what is happening, a number of stylistic conventions have been used throughout this book.

The key styles of text used in this book to distinguish between different types of information are:

- New terms and important words are **bolded**.

- Words you would type are shown as `AZURECURVE\srvc.gp`.

- Key combinations are shown as *Win+R*.

Errata

Every care has been taken to ensure the accuracy of the books content, but mistakes do happen. If you find a mistake in this book we would be grateful if you could report this to us; reporting an error means we can fix the error and improve future editions of the book.

Please report errors by visiting https://publishing.azurecurve.co.uk/submit-errata, select the book in question from the drop down list and enter the details of the errata in the textbox.

Reader Feedback

Feedback from readers is always welcomed as it will enable us to improve future titles. Please let us know what you think about this book, in particular what you liked and disliked.

If you are having problems with any aspect of the book, or have questions about the content you can contact us at questions.book@azurecurve.co.uk.

Piracy

The Internet is a marvelous invention, but it does represent an ongoing problem for the protection of published works. If you happen across any unlicensed copies of our works, in any form, please provide us with the website name or link, so that we can pursue a remedy, by email at copyright@azurecurve.co.uk.

1

Introduction to the Microsoft Dynamics GP Web Client

Microsoft Dynamics GP has, since its inception, been a desktop based client which needed to either be installed on the user's PC or on a Terminal or Citrix Server. Microsoft Dynamics GP 2013 saw the introduction of a new client, a web client, which can be accessed through a Silverlight enabled web browser. Microsoft Dynamics GP 2016 saw the Silverlight web client replaced with an HTML5 one; this new web client is not a replacement to the desktop client, rather it is in complement to it.

Why use the web client?

As technology and connectivity has become more advanced and more robust, distributed working has become more common. "Bring your own device" has also grown in popularity, but this means that IT departments have less control over devices and so security risks have grown.

The web client allows users to log into Microsoft Dynamics GP and do their normal work through the web browser from any device. This means the risks of allowing personal devices to connect to internal networks is removed as, with the web client externally accessible, they only need access to a guest Wi-Fi network.

In addition, the web client is lighter to operate than the desktop client, so more users can use the web client on a single session host than can on a terminal or Citrix server.

Architecture of the Microsoft Dynamics GP Web Client

The Microsoft Dynamics GP **Web Client** consists of eight components used for a single machine or scale-out deployment:

1. IIS **GP Web Site** is the site which web client users will log into. It will serve the aspx pages and **HTML5** web application. The web site will contain a virtual directory named GP. The website must be enabled for **SSL**.

2. IIS **Web Management Console Web Site** is the site administrators will use to manage the web client. This site contains a virtual directory called Web Management Console.

   There will be one, and possibly two, Silverlight applications running in this site.

   The first, which will always be present, is the **Session Management** application which is used to see and manage all of the **Dynamics GP Runtime** processes that are running on any of the session host machines.

   The second is the **Tenant Management** application will is used to manage a multi-tenant deployment.

1. **Session Central Service** is the Windows Service installed on the Web Server. This service communicates with the Web Site as well as the Session Service.

   The Session Central Service collects data from the session hosts and directs new logon requests to the session host which is the most available.

2. **Session Host** is the server which hosts the **Session Service** and one, or more, instances of the Microsoft Dynamics GP 2013 client with the **Web Client Runtime** installed.

   In a scale-out or multi-tenant deployment multiple session hosts would be deployed for load balance and utilization purposes.

3. **Session Service** is the Windows Service running on the Session Host and authorizes users, creates user sessions, retrieves existing sessions and monitors sessions to report back to the Session Central Service.

   The Session Service also starts a shell instance of Microsoft Dynamics GP when a requesting GP Web Client user is authenticated as a valid user.

4. **Session Monitor** is an internal component of the Session Service and runs on a configurable interval to inspect the running sessions, perform any clean up tasks and report the information to the Session Central Service.

5. **GP Runtime Service** is the WCF service which handles the interactions between the GP Web Silverlight application and the Microsoft Dynamics GP Web Client Runtime.

WCF, or the Windows Communication Foundation, is a framework for building service-oriented applications. Using WCF, you can send data as asynchronous messages from one service endpoint to another.

Pros & Cons of the Web Client

The Microsoft Dynamics GP web client is not a replacement to the classic desktop client; rather it is intended to provide another option during the implementation of Microsoft Dynamics GP. An implementation of Microsoft Dynamics GP can be done with one of three types of client installation:

1. Classic desktop client;

2. Web client;

3. Mixture of desktop and web clients.

The main pro of the web client is that it offers the flexibility to access Microsoft Dynamics GP from anywhere, anytime. As it is web based, there is no requirement for users to log in through a VPN, Remote Desktop or Citrix session.

A session host machine can typically host a much larger number of users than a terminal or Citrix server can; according to the system requirements document (see above), 16GB is sufficient to host 120 web client users.

Being web based brings an immediate con (from a certain point of view); the web client is written in Silverlight and is officially supported only in Internet Explorer 8+. So to run in an officially supported configuration you need a Windows based PC or tablet to access the web client.

However, Silverlight is available for Chrome 12+, FireFox 12+ and Safari 4+ which means you can use other browsers, or even other operating systems, as long as you can install Silverlight into the browser. This is not supported by Microsoft, so is an "at your own risk" option.

The web client supports customizations or add-on modules written in either **Dexterity** or **.NET** (both C# and VB.NET), but it does not support customizations done in **Modifier** where they use **Visual Basic for Applications** (VBA). VBA is a quick and easy way of making changes and adding functionality to windows, but this does not look like it will ever make it into the web client.

The web client is meant to compliment the desktop client; indeed they share the same code base (the web client installation on the session host(s) has a desktop client with the Web Client Runtime feature added) and both have seen additional development in Microsoft Dynamics GP 213 R2; the desktop client saw the addition of action panes.

The web client is actually very easy to implement, as we'll see in later chapters, and also scales very well. For light users, such as people raising purchase requisitions or entering Project Accounting or Payroll Timesheets it can be a far better way of accessing Microsoft Dynamics GP.

For users who do mass data entry or produce a lot of reports I would still generally recommend a desktop client be used; the web client is reasonably quick, but is not as quick or responsive as the desktop client.

Deployment Configurations

The Microsoft Dynamics GP web client can be deployed in three ways:

1. Single machine;

2. Scale-out;

3. Multi-tenant.

The **single machine deployment** is the simplest of the deployment configurations available; this deployment has the session central and session host installed on the same machine. A separate SQL Server and Domain Controller are still required in this deployment type; the single machine name of it refers to all of the web client components being installed on the same machine.

The second deployment configuration, and the one this book will cover, is the **scale-out deployment**. This is where there is one or more IIS servers installed as Session Central Servers along with one or more servers installed as Session Hosts depending on the number of web client users and redundancy requirements. This type of deployment is the most flexible for Microsoft Dynamics GP users as it allows additional Session Hosts to be added to the deployment to be quickly and easily added.

The third, and final, deployment configuration is the **multi-tenant deployment**. This is very similar to the scale-out deployment, but is intended for resellers of Microsoft Dynamics GP rather than end users. The multi-tenanted deployment is set up for access by multiple organizations in a hosting environment.

System Requirements

There are three deployment configurations, but only two sets of system requirements Published by Microsoft:

1. Single machine:

2. Scale-Out and Multi-Tenant.

Microsoft maintains an updated system requirements page for every Dynamics GP version. The following URL is specific to Dynamics GP 2018 and the 2019 October Release and requires access to either PartnerSource or CustomerSource:

https://mbs.microsoft.com/customersource/northamerica/GP/learning/documentation /system-requirements/MDGP2018_system_requirements_web_apps

All of this information is updated as new versions and service packs of products are released and tested, so it is important to refer to the current documentation online when planning your web client implementation.

Single Machine Deployment

The web client requirements published by Microsoft are typically the minimums needed to install and run the Microsoft Dynamics GP web client and should sometimes be taken with a pinch of salt. This is especially true when scaling the server for a larger number of users.

Operating System	Microsoft Windows Server 2019 - Datacenter Edition Microsoft Windows Server 2016 - Datacenter Edition Microsoft Windows Server 2012 and 2012 R2 - Datacenter Edition Enterprise Edition or Standard Edition
Processor	1 Quad Core or 2 Dual Core Processors or higher
Minimum Available RAM	4 GB – Up to 25 concurrent web client users 8 GB – Up to 60 concurrent web client users 16 GB – Up to 120 concurrent web client users
Network Card	1GB Ethernet or Fiber
Bandwidth Consideration	Planning Average: 25 Mbps(Megabytes/sec) per active Web Client user with spikes up to 250 Mbps per active Web Client user (see note 5)
Internet Information Services (IIS) (Web Client only)	IIS 10.0 IIS 8.5 IIS 8.0 IIS 7.5
Other Applications	.Net Framework 4.5.1+, 4.6 ASP.Net 4.0+ SQL Native Client 10.0 or 11.0

	Adobe Reader (Required to read or print manuals)

Scale-Out and Multi-Tenant

As already mentioned the scale-out and multi-tenant deployment configurations have the same system requirement and, as with the single machine deployment, the web client requirements published by Microsoft are typically the minimums needed to install and run the Microsoft Dynamics GP web client and should sometimes be taken with a pinch of salt. This is especially true when scaling the server for a larger number of users or, in the case of multi-tenant deployments, the number of organizations.

Web Server(s)

Operating System	Microsoft Windows Server 2019 - Datacenter Edition
	Microsoft Windows Server 2016 - Datacenter Edition
	Microsoft Windows Server 2012 and 2012 R2 - Datacenter Edition
	Enterprise Edition or Standard Edition
Processor	1 Dual Core Processor or higher
Minimum Available RAM	4 GB or more
Network Card	1 GB Ethernet or Fiber
Internet Information Services (IIS) (Web Client only)	IIS 10.0 IIS 8.5 IIS 8.0 IIS 7.5
Other Applications	.Net Framework 4.5.1+, 4.6 ASP.Net 4.0+ SQL Native Client 10.0 or 11.0

Session Server(s)

Operation System	Microsoft Windows Server 2019 - Datacenter Edition
	(18.2.1013 GP version or later)
	Microsoft Windows Server 2016 - Datacenter Edition
	Microsoft Windows Server 2012 and 2012 R2 - Datacenter Edition
	Enterprise Edition or Standard Edition

Processor	1 Quad Core or 2 Dual Core Processors or higher (see note 8)
Minimum Available RAM	4 GB – Up to 25 concurrent web client users 8 GB – Up to 60 concurrent web client users 16 GB – Up to 120 concurrent web client users (for SBA sizing see note 10)
Network Card	1 GB Ethernet or Fiber
Bandwidth Consideration	Planning Average: 25 Mbps(Megabytes/sec) per active Web Client user with spikes up to 250 Mbps per active Web Client user (see note 5)
Other Applications	.NET Framework 4.5.1+, 4.6 SQL Native Client 10.0 or 11.0 Adobe Reader (Required to read or print manuals)

Summary

In this chapter we have introduced the Microsoft Dynamics GP web client and taken a look at the pros and cons of implementing it. This was followed by covering the deployment configurations and their system requirements. In the next chapter we will cover the prerequisites of the Microsoft Dynamics GP Web Client.

2

Prerequisites of the Microsoft Dynamics GP Web Client

Before installing the Microsoft Dynamics GP web client itself, there are a number of prerequisites which need to be installed. In this chapter we'll take a run through the prerequisites for both the session central and session host components; in the case of a single machine deployment, these components will both be installed on the same machine.

Install the .NET Framework 4.5 (or later) Features

If you're using Windows Server 2012, or later, the **.NET Framework 4.5 Features** cannot be installed by the **Microsoft Dynamics GP Bootstrapper Setup** utility. Instead they need to be enabled via the **Server Manager**:

1. Launch **Server Manager** and select **Add roles and features**.

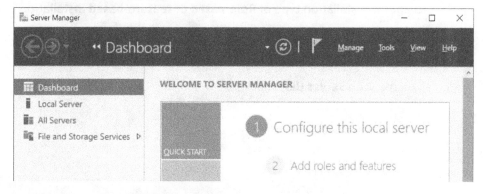

2. On the **Before you begin** page click **Next**.

3. Accept the installation type of **Role-based or feature-based installation** and click **Next**.

4. Select the server the feature is to be installed on and click **Next**.

5. Click **Features** and mark the **.NET Framework 4.5 Features** checkbox.

6. Click **Next**.

7. If you have an Internet connection available on the server click *Install*; if there is not one then click the **Specify an alternative source path** link. Enter the **Path** of the installation files, click *OK* and then click **Install**.

8. Once the **.NET Framework 4.5 Feature** is installed, click **Close**.

This feature needs to be installed on all of the session central and session host servers.

Installing the Web Server (IIS) Role

The Web Server (IIS) role is required on each of the session central servers of the scale-out deployment. The Web Server role is installed via Server Manager:

1. Launch **Server Manager** and select **Add roles and features**.

2. On the **Before you begin** page click **Next**.

3. Accept the installation type of **Role-based or feature-based installation** and click **Next**.

4. Select the server the feature is to be installed on and click **Next**.

5. Mark the **Web Server (IIS)** checkbox.

Select one or more roles to install on the selected server.

Roles

- [ ] Active Directory Domain Services
- [ ] Active Directory Federation Services
- [ ] Active Directory Lightweight Directory Services
- [ ] Active Directory Rights Management Services
- [ ] Device Health Attestation
- [ ] DHCP Server
- [ ] DNS Server
- [ ] Fax Server
- [■] File and Storage Services (1 of 12 installed)
- [ ] Host Guardian Service
- [ ] Hyper-V
- [ ] Network Controller
- [ ] Network Policy and Access Services
- [ ] Print and Document Services
- [ ] Remote Access
- [ ] Remote Desktop Services
- [ ] Volume Activation Services
- [✓] Web Server (IIS)
- [ ] Windows Deployment Services
- [ ] Windows Server Update Services

6. A pop-up box will be displayed listing a set of tools which are required to manage the IIS feature; they do not need to be installed if you already have them installed elsewhere. Click **Add Features** to install the tools or **Cancel** if you have them elsewhere.

7. Click **Next** twice to progress to the **Role Services** step.

8. Expand the **Web Server** and **Security** nodes and then mark **Windows Authentication**.

Select the role services to install for Web Server (IIS)

Role services

- [ ] Dynamic Content Compression
- ▲ [✓] Security
  - [✓] Request Filtering
  - [ ] Basic Authentication
  - [ ] Centralized SSL Certificate Support
  - [ ] Client Certificate Mapping Authentication
  - [ ] Digest Authentication
  - [ ] IIS Client Certificate Mapping Authenticatic
  - [ ] IP and Domain Restrictions
  - [ ] URL Authorization
  - [✓] Windows Authentication
- ▷ [ ] Application Development

9. Click **Next** and then on the **Confirm installation selections** page click **Install**.

10. Once the installation of **Web Server (IIS)** is complete click **Close**.

With the **Web Server (IIS)** role installed the next step is to decide which web sites are to be used for the web client. You can:

1. Use the **Default Web Site** for both the **Web Client** and **Web Management Console**;

2. Create a new web site to host both the **Web Client** and **Web Management Console**;

3. Use the **Default Web Site** for one and create a new site for the other;

4. Create two new web sites.

For the deployments I am covering in this book, I have chosen to use the first option; I am using the **Default Web Site** for both the **Web Client** and the **Web Management Console**. In later chapters I will point out where I am doing this and what you need to do if you are using two web sites.

Add HTTP Activation to .NET Framework 4.5 Features

For the Microsoft Dynamics GP web management console to function, the **HTTP Activation** feature needs to be added to the **.NET Framework 4.5 Features**:

1. Launch **Server Manager** and select **Add roles and features**.

2. On the **Before you begin** page click **Next**.

3. Accept the installation type of **Role-based or feature-based installation** and click **Next**.

4. Expand **.NET Framework 4.5 Features** and then **WCF Services**.

5. Mark **HTTP Activation**.

6. As this feature has dependencies on other roles or features, a dialog will be displayed listing these dependencies and confirmation that they should be displayed. Click **Add Features** to add **HTTP Activation** and all required role services and features.

7. Click **Next** and then click **Install**..

8. Once the installation is complete, click **Close**.

Bind a Security Certificate

As with all secure web facing systems, the Microsoft Dynamics GP web client needs to be secured with an **SSL certificate**. The best option is to install a **wildcard certificate** on each of the session central and session host servers; if individual certificates are used then each server will need the certificate of all others importing in the **Internet Information Services (IIS) Manager** (select the server and then under *IIS* on the area page double click on **Server Certificates**).

Wildcard SSL certificates range in cost depending on the organization they are bought from. For example, from RapidSSL one costs $59/year (http://www.rapidssl.com) whereas GoDaddy charges $79/year (http://www.godaddy.com).

Once you have the certificate installed, perform the following steps to bind the certificate to the website:

1. Open **Internet Information Services (IIS) Manager**.

2. Select the server hosting the website and expand the **Sites** node.

3. Right click on the website and select **Edit Bindings...**

4. Click **Add...** to add a new binding.

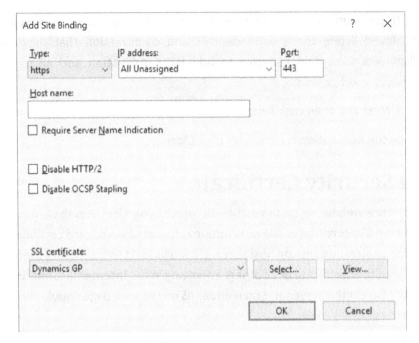

5. Set the *Type* to **https** and change the port to the one you want to run the website under; **443** is the typical port used for a website running on https.

6. In the **SSL certificate** dropdown select the required certificate; in my case the certificate was imported with a friendly name of **Dynamics GP**.

7. Click *OK*.

8. Click **Close** to close the **Site Bindings** window.

9. Close **Internet Information Services (IIS) Manager**.

Before closing the **Site Bindings** window you could remove the **port 80 binding** so the site will only be listening on **port 443**. Rather than doing this I will often look at setting up a redirect from the **http** to the **https** binding so users don't need to worry about typing the exact address.

Externally accessible DNS entry

To allow for external access to the web client, an externally accessible DNS entry is required. For example, to use my blog domain **azurecurve.co.uk** as an example, I might create a domain for the web client called **msdyngp**. This would allow users to type https://msdyngp.azurecurve.co.uk/GP to access the web client in the browser.

Open Ports

There are four ports which will need to be open for users to use the web client; however, only the port used by the website will need to be open on the external firewall. The other ports only need to be open internally for the components of the web client to communicate between servers (this only applied to a scale-out deployment).

Create Active Directory User Groups

The web client uses **Windows User Groups** for determining which users can access the web client and the web management console. **User Groups** provide an easy and quick way of granting additional users access to the Microsoft Dynamics GP web client.

There is two user groups required; one for the users who will log into Microsoft Dynamics GP using the web client and one for the system administrators who will use the web management console.

To create a **Windows User Group** for the web client, perform the following steps:

1. Log onto the **Domain Controller**.

2. Open **Active Directory Users and Computers** from the **Control Panel**.

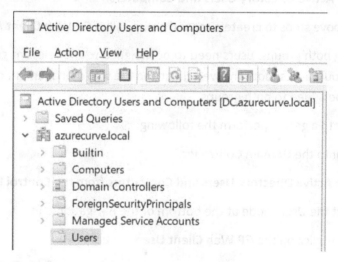

3. Select the **Users** node at the bottom of the navigation pane.

4. Click the **Create a new group in the current container** button on the toolbar.

5. Enter **GP Web Client Users** in the **Group name** field and click **OK**.

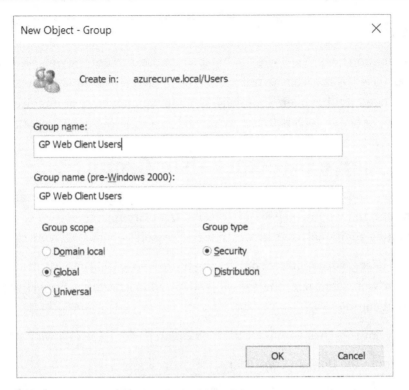

6. Close **Active Directory Users and Computers**.

Repeat the above steps to create a second group called **GP Web Client Admins**.

After creating both groups, users need to be assigned to the relevant group. If you have a user who would access both the web client and the web management console then they will need to be added to both groups.

To add a user to a group, perform the following:

1. Log onto the **Domain Controller**.

2. Open **Active Directory Users and Computers** from the **Control Panel**.

3. Select the **Users** node at the bottom of the navigation pane.

4. Double click on the **GP Web Client Users** group.

5. Select the **Members** tab.

6. Click the **Add...** button, enter a user's name and click **Check Names**.

7. The users **Name** and **Domain logon** will be displayed.

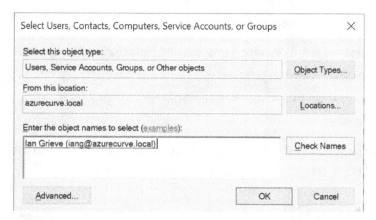

8. click **OK** to add the user to the group.

9. Repeat steps 6 through 8 until all required users have been added.

10. Click **OK** to close the **GP Web Client Users Properties** dialog.

11. Repeat steps 4 through to 9 for the **GP Web Client Admins** group.

12. Close **Active Directory Users and Computers**.

Only the users in the Windows User Groups will be able to log into the Microsoft Dynamics GP web client or web management console. You do not have to create new groups for use with the Web Client. Existing Groups can be used should the appropriate groups already exist.

At some clients, the **Domain Administrators** group has been used as the **Web Management Console** users group.

You can also use multiple groups for both the Web Client Users and Web Management Console Users should you wish to do so.

Required User Accounts

An implementation of the Microsoft Dynamics GP web client requires a number of user accounts to run the web site and services.

Security best practice requires the service accounts have limited privileges assigned and a password which does not expire. It is strongly recommended that you create all of the user accounts before starting to install the web client.

There are four services for which user accounts are required:

1. **Web Client site application pool** - this account runs the application pool for the web site that hosts the web client.

2. **Web Management Console application pool** - this account runs the application

---

pool for the web site that hosts the web client.

3. **Session Central Service** – this account runs the Session Central Service on the web server.

4. **Session Service** – this account runs the Session Service on each session host machine.

The web client and Web Management Console can be deployed to the same web site in which case only one application pool user account is required.

Dynamics GP

Last, but by no means least, before any web client deployment is done, Microsoft Dynamics GP itself needs to be installed and configured on the session host machines.

If you are implementing a brand new Microsoft Dynamics GP system then you also need to have installed one client and deployed the system database and created at least one company (or installed the sample company).

Summary

Now that we have the prerequisites for the session central and session host servers installed, in the next chapter we'll take a look at installing an Microsoft Dynamics GP web client scale-out deployment.

3

Microsoft Dynamics GP Web Client Single Machine Deployment

Now that we have the prerequisites of the Microsoft Dynamics GP web client installed, we can focus on the deployment. As mentioned in ***Chapter 1, Introduction to the Microsoft Dynamics GP Web Client*** there are three deployment methods, in this chapter we're going to take a look at the single machine deployment. This is where there is a single machine running all of the web client components.

Installing the Web Client Components

The Microsoft Dynamics GP web client is installed from the same Microsoft Dynamics GP **setup utility** as the desktop client. Run the setup.exe on the installation media to begin the installation.

Before the setup utility itself is displayed the **Microsoft Dynamics GP Bootstrapper Setup** will appear and show the prerequisites which need to be installed; click on **Install** to install the prerequisites.

A reboot of the server may be required after the prerequisites have been installed. It is recommend that this be done before proceeding with the main part of the installation.

Once they have been installed, the **Microsoft Dynamics GP setup utility** window will be displayed. To install the session central components of the web client, perform the following steps:

1. Under **Additional Products** click on **Web Client**.

2. Read and accept the **License Agreement**, then click on **Next** to continue.

3. Next you will be shown the **Installation Option** where we need to select **Custom**; the **Single Machine** option will actually install other web components which are not required for the web client.

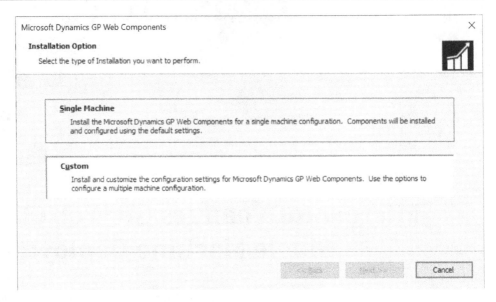

4. Change the **Service Based Architecture** feature to not installed; all of the items under **Web Server** should be selected with the exception of **SBA Session** Manager and **Tenant Manager**.

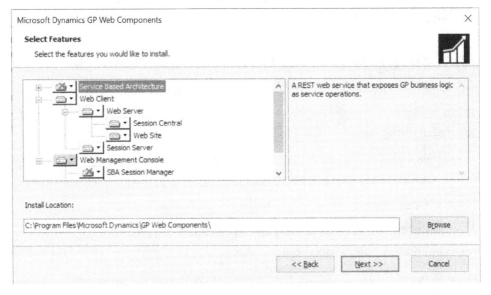

5. If required, change the **Install Location** if the Windows default program files location should not be used.

6. Click **Next** to continue.

7. The **Session Central Database** location and connection details need to be supplied:

    i.   The **Server Name** should include the **SQL Server Instance Name** if a Named Instance is being used. In my test system I am using a server called

> **SQL2019** and a Named Instance called **GP** so I have entered SQL2019\GP.

ii. The **Database Name** will default to **GPCONFIGURATION**, but this can be changed if necessary.

iii. You can use **Windows Authentication** if the user you are logged in with has the required permissions on the SQL Server, although I typically prefer to use **SQL Authentication** and the sa account to ensure all required permissions are present.

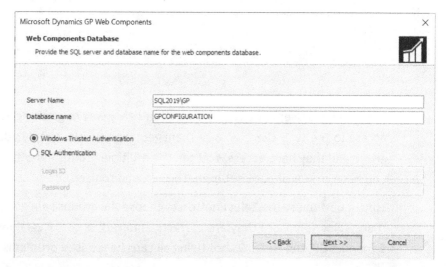

iv. If using **SQL Authentication** supply the Login ID and Password.

8. Click **Next** to continue.

9. On the **Authentication Type** step, leave this set to Windows Account if you're using on-premise Active Directory; if using Azure, change it to **Organization Account** or **Mixed Mode** and enter your Azure Organizational Settings.

10. On the **Windows User Group** step you need to define the group(s) containing the web client and web management console users (these would be the groups created in the Prerequisites chapter); when entering the groups ensure the Domain is prefixed.

11. The Windows User Groups give a quick and easy way of granting additional users access to the web client or web management console; simply add them to the group and they have access. You can use multiple groups in both sections should you have groups already setup that you intend to use.

    I find it best to use the **Select** button to choose the groups I am going to use rather than typing to ensure they are correctly entered; in some versions of Microsoft Dynamics GP, the NETBIOS not being all caps has caused problems.

    Once you have entered the required groups, click **Next**.

12. The **Tenant Configuration** stage can be ignored as we are focusing on doing a scale-out deployment and this stage is only required for multi-tenant deployments. Click Next.

13. On the **GP Configuration** step you will need to supply the username and password the web client will use to connect to the GP databases; this should be the same username and password used during the installation of the Dynamics GP client.

    If the **SQL Server Login Name** does not exist then a password confirmation will be displayed after the password is entered. This information will be used to create a new login in SQL with the required permissions; if the user does exist then the permissions will be updated.

14. If Microsoft Dynamics GP is going to be installed on the session hosts in a non-standard location then make sure to update the **Dynamics GP runtime Folder**, **Path to Dynamics.set** and **Path to Dex.ini** paths.

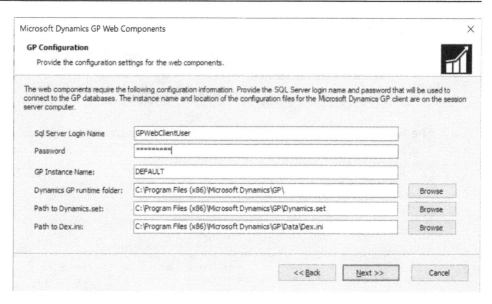

15. Click **Next** to continue.

16. Next we need to define the settings for the **Session Central Service**:

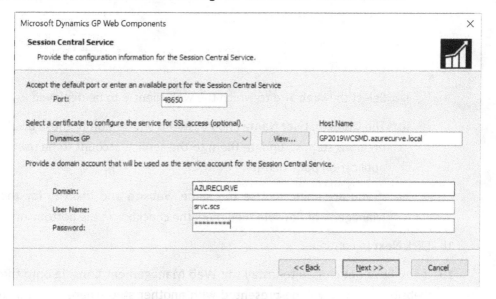

i. The port will default to *48650*; change this if required, but make sure which ever port is being used has an exception defined in the firewall.

ii. Choose the certificate to configure the service for SSL access.

Depending on the certificate you may need to enter the host name (this should be set to the fully qualified domain name of the server. If using a wildcard certificate, remove the comma and everything following.

For this book I am using a self-signed certificate and the server is called **GP2019WCSMD** and is joined to the **azurecurve.local** domain, so I have entered GP2019WCSMD.azurecurve.local.

    iii. Enter the **Domain**, **User Name** and **Password** that will be used for the **Session Central Service**.

    iv. Click **Next** to proceed.

17. The **Web Site Configuration** is the next step in the deployment process:

    i. Select the **Web Site** to which the web client is to be deployed.

    ii. The **Domain**, **User Name** and **Password** will default to those used on the previous step, so update them to the service account to be used for the application pool identity.

    iii. If you are going to **Use the same website and identity for the Web Management Console** then mark the checkbox in the bottom left corner.

18. Click **Next** to continue.

19. If you have not chosen to install the **Web Management Console** onto the same website then you will be presented with another step where you will select a website and enter the application pool identity account; I did choose to use the same website so did not see this step.

20. If you are implementing the scale-out deployment on a large client site then you may want to deploy the session central to multiple web servers. This is done on the **Web Server Farm Configuration** step by marking the **Deploy on multiple web servers** checkbox and completing the details.

In this book, we are not covering a multiple web server deployment so I have not marked this checkbox.

21. Click **Next** to continue.

22. We need to define the settings for the **Session Service**:

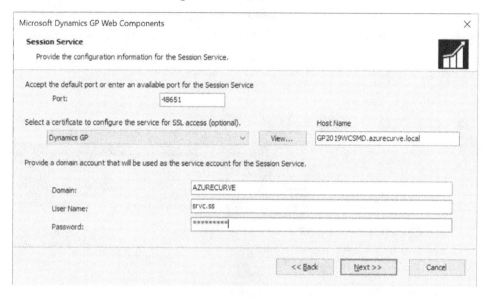

    i.   The port will default to *48651*; change this if required, but make sure which ever port is being used has an exception defined in the firewall.

    ii.   Choose the certificate to configure the service for SSL access.

        Depending on the certificate you may need to enter the host name (this should be set to the fully qualified domain name of the server. If using a wildcard certificate, remove the comma and everything following.

        For this book I am using a self-signed certificate and the server is called **GP2019WCSMD** and is joined to the **azurecurve.local** domain, so I have entered GP2019WCSMD.azurecurve.local.

    iii.   The **Domain**, **User Name** and **Password** will default to the ones entered for the session central service; change them to the domain account which will be used for the **Session Service**.

    iv.   Click **Next** to proceed.

23. The Runtime Service URL needs to be configured next:

    i.   The port should be set to the same one bound to the website.

    ii.   Choose the certificate to configure the service for SSL access.

        Depending on the certificate you may need to enter the host name (this should be set to the fully qualified domain name of the server. If using a wildcard certificate, remove the comma and everything following.

For this book I am using a self-signed certificate and the server is called **GP2019WCSMD** and is joined to the **azurecurve.local** domain, so I have entered `GP2019WCSMD.azurecurve.local`.

24. Click **Next** to continue.

25. The final step is the installation confirmation one which invites you to review the installation settings; unfortunately, this step doesn't actually show you the settings you entered.

    i.   If you need to check the settings use the *Back* button to step back through the settings and **Next** to move forward again.

    ii. When happy, click **Install** to start the installation.

26. Once the install has finished the **Installation Complete** step will be displayed where you can click **Exit** to close the installer.

At this point, the **Microsoft Dynamics GP Web Client Configuration Wizard** will automatically be started which will allow you to create the required databases:

1. Click **Next** to start the configuration.

2. For the **SQL Connection Information** for the Web Management Console, choose the authentication method and, if using **SQL Authentication**, enter the **User Name** and **Password**.

   The **Server Name** and **Database Name** fields will show the values entered during the installation.

3. Click **Next** to continue.

4. The **Configuration Status and Actions** step will confirm if the databases exist or not. For a standard scale-out deployment they won't so clicking **Next** will create them; if you're installing multiple web servers then subsequent servers will connect to the existing databases.

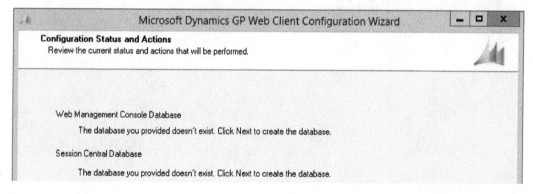

5. Once the databases have been created and populated a confirmation step, **Configuration Complete**, will be displayed. Click **Exit**.

A second program, **Microsoft Dynamics GP Web Client Help**, was also automatically started alongside the **Microsoft Dynamics GP Web Client Configuration Wizard**:

1. Click **Install** to begin the installation process.

2. There is no user input needed to install the help files; click **Finish** when it has completed.

With the session central service installed on the web server(s) the next step is to install at least one session host.

Installing the client features and components

In this section I am assuming that you already have the Microsoft Dynamics GP client installed on the machine hosting the single machine deployment. What we will cover here is adding the **Web Client Runtime** to the desktop client and then installing the **GP Web Resource Cache**.

To add the **Web Client Runtime**, start the **Add or remove programs** routine in **Control Panel** (hit *Win+R* and type **appwiz.cpl** for quick access):

1. Select **Microsoft Dynamics GP**and then click **Change**.

2. Click **Add/Remove Features**.

3. Scroll to the bottom of the features list and change **Web Client Runtime to Run from my computer**.

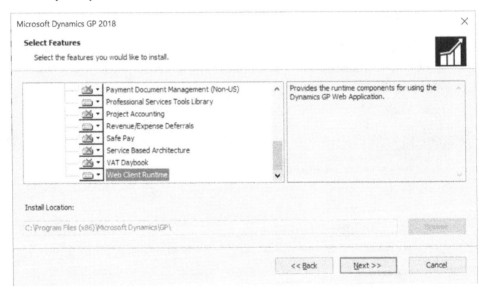

4. Click **Next**.

5. Click **Install** to begin the installation.

6. When the install has completed, click **Exit** and close the **Program and Features** window.

With the desktop client updated to have the **Web Client Runtime** the next step is to install the **GP Web Resource Cache**. To do this run the **setup.exe** on the installation media to begin the installation.

To install the **GP Web Resource Cache** component of the web client, perform the following steps:

1. Under **Additional Products** click on **GP Web Resource Cache**.

2. On the **Welcome** step, click on **Install**.

3. Once the installation is complete, click **Exit** to close the installer.

With the **GP Web Resource Cache** installed, the web client is not ready for use. I'll cover this in *chapter 4, Using the Microsoft Dynamics GP Web Client*.

Summary

In this chapter we have installed a single machine deployment of the Microsoft Dynamics GP web client. In the next chapter, we'll take a look at installing a scale-out deployment of the web client.

4

Microsoft Dynamics GP Web Client Scale-Out Deployment

Now that we have the prerequisites of the Microsoft Dynamics GP web client installed, we can focus on the deployment. As mentioned in *Chapter 1, Introduction to the Microsoft Dynamics GP Web Client* there are three deployment methods, in this chapter we're going to take a look at the most common of the deployment methods; the scale-out deployment. This is where there are multiple session host machines (and possibly multiple web servers as well).

Installing the Session Central Server

The Microsoft Dynamics GP web client is installed from the same Microsoft Dynamics GP **setup utility** as the desktop client. Run the setup.exe on the installation media to begin the installation.

Before the setup utility itself is displayed the **Microsoft Dynamics GP Bootstrapper Setup** will appear and show the prerequisites which need to be installed; click on **Install** to install the prerequisites.

A reboot of the server may be required after the prerequisites have been installed. It is recommend that this be done before proceeding with the main part of the installation.

Once they have been installed, the **Microsoft Dynamics GP setup utility** window will be displayed. To install the session central components of the web client, perform the following steps:

1. Under **Additional Products** click on **Web Client**.

2. Read and accept the **License Agreement**, then click on **Next** to continue.

3. Next you will be shown the **Installation Option** where, for a **scale-out deployment**, we need to select **Custom**.

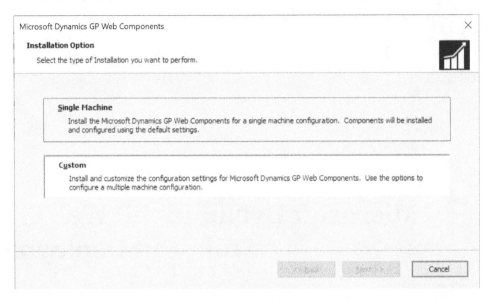

4. Set the entire **Service Based Architecture** feature to not available; change the **Session Server** option to not installed; only **Web Client Session Manager** under **Web Management Console** should be selected.

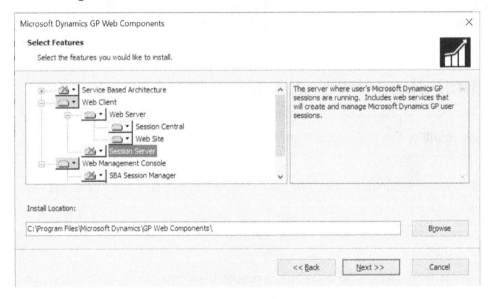

5. If required, change the **Install Location** if the Windows default program files location should not be used.

6. Click **Next** to continue.

7. For the **Web Components Database** step, supply the **Server Name** (including instance name if your SQL Server is a Named Instance) and the **Database Name** which will default to GPCONFIGURATION, but can be changed (as I have done).

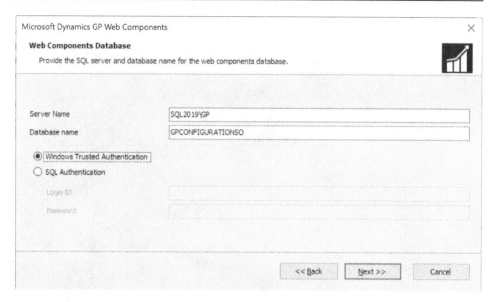

8. As with the Web Client Database select the authentication method and supply the **Login ID** and **Password** if using **SQL Authentication**.

   Before proceeding, make sure that the selected user has the necessary permissions to create a database on the SQL Server.

9. Click **Next** to continue.

10. On the **Authentication Type** step, leave this set to Windows Account if you're using on-premise Active Directory; if using Azure, change it to **Organization Account** or **Mixed Mode** and enter your Azure Organizational Settings.

11. Click **Next** to continue.

12. On the **Windows User Group** step you need to define the group(s) containing the web client and web management console users (these would be the groups created in the Prerequisites chapter); when entering the groups ensure the Domain is prefixed.

13. The Windows User Groups give a quick and easy way of granting additional users access to the web client or web management console; simply add them to the group and they have access. You can use multiple groups in both sections should you have groups already setup that you intend to use.

   I find it best to use the **Select** button to choose the groups I am going to use rather than typing to ensure they are correctly entered; in the Microsoft Dynamics GP 2013 beta the Domain not being all caps caused problems.

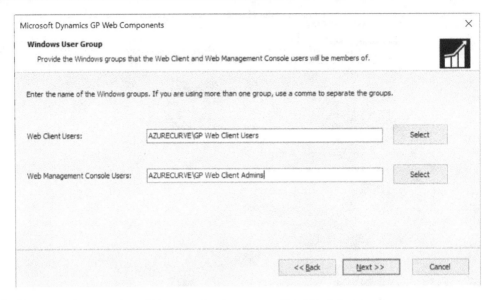

14. Once you have entered the required groups, click **Next**.

15. The **Tenant Configuration** stage can be ignored as we are focusing on doing a scale-out deployment and this stage is only required for multi-tenant deployments. Click **Next**.

16. On the **GP Configuration** step you will need to supply the username and password the web client will use to connect to the GP databases; if the **SQL Server Login Name** does not exist then a password confirmation will be displayed after the password is entered. This information will be used to create a new login in SQL with the required permissions; if the user does exist then the permissions will be updated.

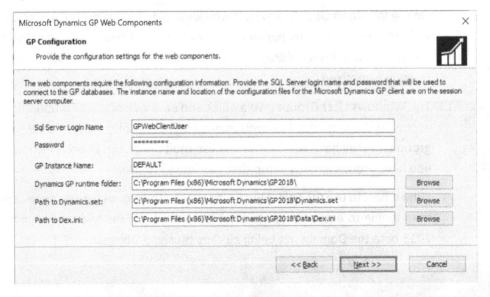

If Microsoft Dynamics GP is going to be installed on the session hosts in a non-standard location then make sure to update the **Dynamics GP runtime Folder**, **Path to Dynamics.set** and **Path to Dex.ini** paths.

17. Click **Next** to continue.

18. Next we need to define the settings for the **Session Central Service**:

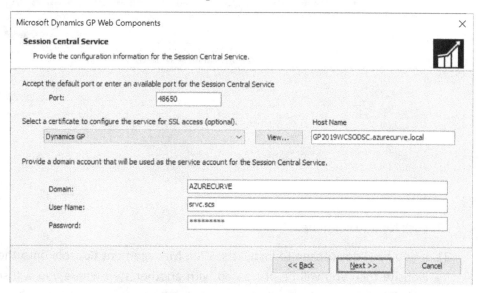

i. The port will default to *48650*; change this if required, but make sure which ever port is being used has an exception defined in the firewall.

ii. Choose the certificate to configure the service for SSL access.

Depending on the certificate you may need to enter the host name (this should be set to the fully qualified domain name of the server; in the example above server is called **GP2019WCSODSC** and is on the Domain **azurecurve.local** so I have entered `GP2019WCSODSC.azurecurve.locaL`.

iii. Enter the **Domain**, **User Name** and **Password** that will be used for the **Session Central Service**.

iv. Click **Next** to proceed.

19. The **Web Site Configuration** is the next step in the deployment process:

i. Select the **Web Site** to which the web client is to be deployed.

ii. The **Domain, User Name** and **Password** will default to those entered for the session central service; to follow best practice, change them to the service account to be used for the application pool identity.

iii. If you are going to **Use the same website and identity for the Web**

Management Console then mark the checkbox in the bottom left corner.

20. Click **Next** to continue.

21. If you have not chosen to install the **Web Management Console** onto the same website then you will be presented with another step where you will select a website and enter the application pool identity account; I did choose to use the same website so did not see this step.

22. If you are implementing the scale-out deployment on a large client site then you may want to deploy the session central to multiple web servers. This is done on the **Web Server Farm Configuration** step by marking the **Deploy on multiple web servers** checkbox and completing the details.

    In this book, we are not covering a multiple web server deployment so I have not marked this checkbox.

23. Click **Next** to continue.

24. The final step is the installation confirmation one which invites you to review the installation settings; unfortunately, this step doesn't actually show you the settings you entered.

    iii. If you need to check the settings use the *Back* button to step back through the settings and **Next** to move forward again.

    iv. When happy, click **Install** to start the installation.

25. Once the install has finished the **Installation Complete** step will be displayed where you can click **Exit** to close the installer.

At this point, the **Microsoft Dynamics GP Web Client Configuration Wizard** will automatically be started which will allow you to create the required databases:

6. Click **Next** to start the configuration.

    For the **SQL Connection Information** for the Web Management Console, the **Server Name** and **Database Name** fields will show the values entered during the installation.

    Select the authentication method and, if using **SQL Authentication**, enter the **User Name** and **Password**.

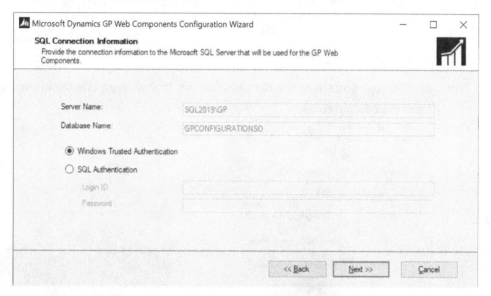

7. Click **Next** to continue.

8. The **Configuration Status and Actions** step will confirm if the databases exist or not. For a standard scale-out deployment they won't so clicking **Next** will create them; if you're installing multiple web servers then subsequent servers will connect to the existing databases.

9. Once the databases have been created and populated a confirmation step, **Configuration Complete**, will be displayed. Click **Exit**.

A second program, **Microsoft Dynamics GP Web Client Help**, was also automatically started alongside the **Microsoft Dynamics GP Web Client Configuration Wizard**:

3. Click **Install** to begin the installation process.

4. There is no user input needed to install the help files; click **Finish** when it has completed.

With the session central service installed on the web server(s) the next step is to install at least one session host.

Installing the Session Hosts

In this section I am assuming that you already have the Microsoft Dynamics GP client installed on the session host machine. What we will cover here is adding the **Web Client Runtime** to the desktop client and then installing the **Session Host Service**.

The steps covered in this section need to be repeated for each of the session host servers.

To add the **Web Client Runtime**, start the **Add or remove programs** routine in **Control Panel** (hit *Win+R* and type **appwiz.cpl** for quick access):

7. Select **Microsoft Dynamics GP** and then click **Change**.

8. Click **Add/Remove Features**.

9. Scroll to the bottom of the features list and change **Web Client Runtime to Run from my computer**.

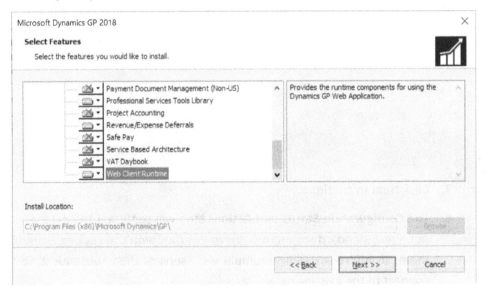

10. Click **Next**.

11. Click **Install** to begin the installation.

12. When the install has completed, click **Exit** and close the **Program and Features** window.

With the desktop client updated to have the **Web Client Runtime** the next step is to install the **Session Host**. To do this run the **setup.exe** on the installation media to begin the installation.

To install the **session host** components of the web client, perform the following steps:

4.   Under **Additional Products** click on **Web Client**;

5. Read and accept the **License Agreement**, then click on **Next** to continue;

6. Next you will be shown the **Installation Options** where, for a **scale-out deployment**, we need to select **Custom**.

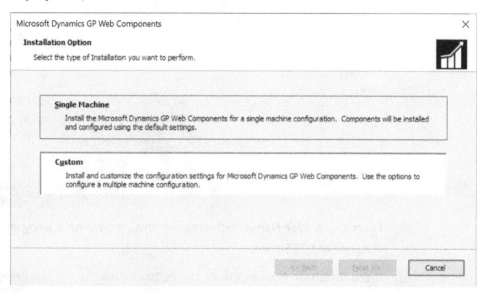

7. Change everything to not available, except the **Session** Server under **Web Server** feature.

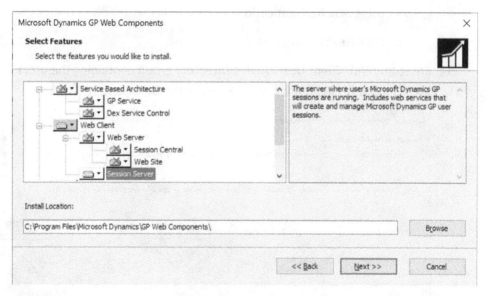

8. If installing to a non-standard location change the **Install Location**; make sure all session host servers are installed to the same location.

9. Click **Next** to proceed.

10. Define the location and login details for the **Session Central Database** created when the **Session Central** was installed:

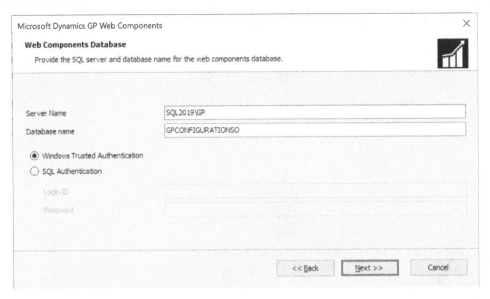

i. Enter the **Server Name**, including the Instance Name if using a Named Instance of SQL Server.

ii. If the **Database Name** default of GPCONFIGURATION is not being used enter the new database name.

iii. Choose the authentication method and the **Login ID** and **Password** if using **SQL Authentication**.

iv. Click **Next** to continue.

11. Enter the **Web Client Users** Active Directory group containing the users who will access the web client; if typing it in ensure the Domain is included.

12. The **Tenant Configuration** stage can be ignored as we are focusing on doing a

scale-out deployment and this stage is only required for multi-tenant deployments. Click Next.

13. Next we need to define the **Session Service** configuration:

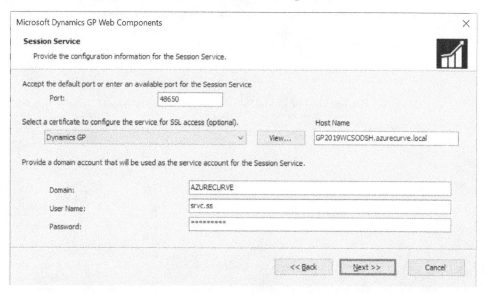

i. The Port will default to 48650, but can be changed if necessary; make sure the port being used has an exception defined in the firewall.

ii. Choose the certificate to use to configure the service for SSL access.

Depending on the certificate you may need to enter the host name (this should be set to the fully qualified domain name of the server; in this example, the server is called **GP2019WCSODSH** and is on the Domain **azurecurve.local** so I have entered GP2019WCSODSH.azurecurve .local.

iii. Enter the **Domain**, **User Name** and **Password** that should be used for the Session Service and click *Next*.

iv. Specify the **Port** which should be used to access the runtime service on this server.

14. Click **Next** to continue.

15. The Runtime Service URL needs to be configured next:

i. The port should be set to the same one bound to the website.

ii. Choose the certificate to configure the service for SSL access.

Depending on the certificate you may need to enter the host name (this should be set to the fully qualified domain name of the server. If using a wildcard certificate, remove the comma and everything following.

For this book I am using a self-signed certificate and the server is called **GP2019WCSODSH** and is joined to the **azurecurve.local** domain, so I have entered `GP2019WCSODSH.azurecurve.local`.

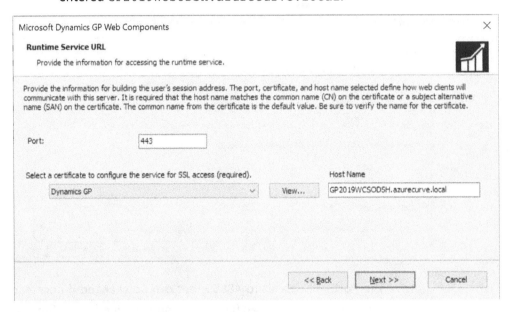

16. Click **Next** to continue.

17. Review you settings, although like the session central installer you don't get presented with the selected options. Click **Install** to begin the installation.

18. Once the installation is complete, click **Exit** to close the installer.

The **Microsoft Dynamics GP Web Client Configuration Wizard** will be started automatically:

1. Click **Next** to proceed with the configuration.

2. The **Server Name** and **Database** will default in from the session service installation.

3. Choose the authentication method and, if using **SQL Authentication**, enter the **User Name** and **Password**.

4. Click **Next** to continue.

5. If you have the settings correct, a step will be displayed stating that the database provided is at the current version.

6. Click **Next**.

7. Click **Exit** to close the **Configuration Wizard**.

This completes the web client installation on the first session host server; repeat on all other servers to be used as session hosts. Additional session hosts don't all need to be installed at once; they can be added at any point required to scale up the number of users who can use the web client to access Microsoft Dynamics GP.

Installing the client features and components

In this section I am assuming that you already have the Microsoft Dynamics GP client installed on the machine hosting the single machine deployment. What we will cover here is adding the **Web Client Runtime** to the desktop client and then installing the **GP Web Resource Cache**.

To add the **Web Client Runtime**, start the **Add or remove programs** routine in **Control Panel** (hit *Win+R* and type **appwiz.cpl** for quick access):

1. Select **Microsoft Dynamics GP**and then click **Change**.

2. Click **Add/Remove Features**.

3. Scroll to the bottom of the features list and change **Web Client Runtime to Run from my computer**.

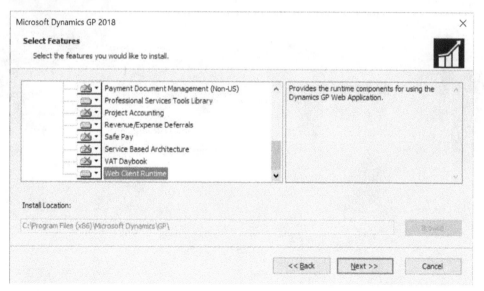

4. Click **Next**.

5. Click **Install** to begin the installation.

6. When the install has completed, click **Exit** and close the **Program and Features** window.

With the desktop client updated to have the **Web Client Runtime** the next step is to install the **GP Web Resource Cache**. To do this run the **setup.exe** on the installation media to begin the installation.

To install the **GP Web Resource Cache** component of the web client, perform the following steps:

1. Under **Additional Products** click on **GP Web Resource Cache**.

2. On the **Welcome** step, click on **Install**.

3. Once the installation is complete, click **Exit** to close the installer.

With the **GP Web Resource Cache** installed, the web client is not ready for use. I'll cover this in *chapter 4, Using the Microsoft Dynamics GP Web Client*.

Summary

In this chapter we have covered the installation of the session central and session host components in a scale-out deployment. In the next chapter, we'll take a look at logging into the web client, the differences between the web and desktop clients and how the web client can be managed.

5

Using the
Microsoft Dynamics GP Web Client

In the previous two chapters we have implemented a single machine and scale-out deployments of the Microsoft Dynamics GP web client. In this chapter, we'll take a look at the process of logging in, have an overview of the key differences between the desktop and web clients, the integration with Microsoft Office and cover how the web client can be managed.

Creating a Web Client Only User

As of Microsoft Dynamics GP 2013 R2, users can be created as Web Client only users. Users are still created through the standard **User Setup** window (Administration area page >> Setup >> System >> User).

When a user is defined as a web client only user, an **SQL Server Account** is not necessary as the SQL login will be done using the **SQL Server Login Name** provided on the **GP Configuration** step during the installation of the **Session Central** on the web server.

What is needed is the Windows Account which the user will log in with. To do this perform the following steps:

1. Click on the **Windows Account** tab to change the bottom section of the window.

2. Click the magnifying glass next to the **Windows Account** field.

3. In the **Windows Account Lookup** window, enter the user name, or part thereof, and click the binoculars icon to perform a lookup on Active Directory users.

4. Select the required **Windows Account** and click **OK**.

5. Click **Save** to save the new user.

A user account created as a web client user will not be able to log into the Microsoft

Dynamics GP desktop client, as there is no **SQL Server Account** associated with it.

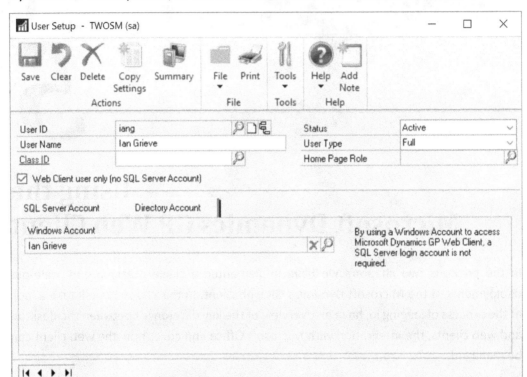

Logging into the Web Client

Early versions of the web client used Microsoft Silverlight, but modern versions are HTML5+CSS and are cross-browser compatible. To access the web client, launch your browser of choice and navigate to https://[domainname]/GP (where [domainname] is the externally accessible DNS entry) where you will be prompted for your Windows domain user account and password; make sure you remember to enter the NETBIOS before your username; to access it on the deployment just installed, I would enter AZURECURVE\iang.

The domain user you log in as must be a member of the Web Client User domain group.

There is an option to choose between whether the computer is a public or shared computer or if it is private. If the computer is private there is a **Remember my user name and password** checkbox available which will allow users to automatically log into the web client without needing to enter their user name and password again.

The login process is somewhat different if the domain user account is connected with a web client only user account in Microsoft Dynamics GP.

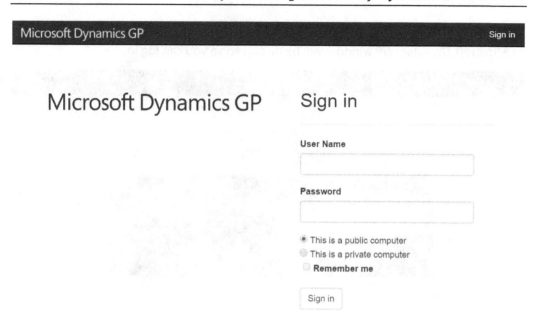

After the web client has loaded, you will, if you have access to more than one company, be presented with the standard *Company Login* window to log in as a GP user, otherwise you will be logged into the single company to which you have access.

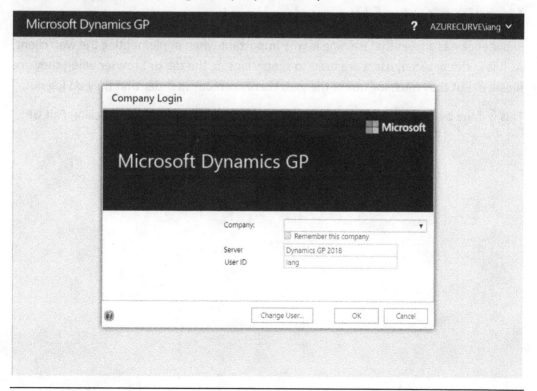

If you are logging in with a user which is not a web client only one, the standard *Welcome to Microsoft Dynamics GP* window will be displayed so you can log in.

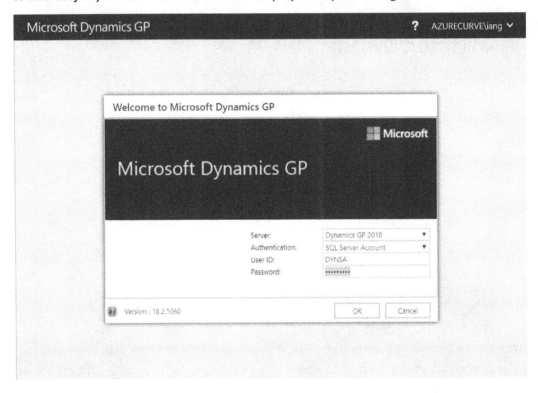

Logging out of the web client

Experience has shown that training is very important when implementing the web client. As it is in the browser, users are used to simply closing the tab or browser when they are finished. But they must log out of the web client correctly in order that they *do* log out.

This is done by clicking their username in the top right corner and then clicking **Exit GP**:

What doesn't work in the web client

Even in version one of the Microsoft Dynamics GP web client, there was little that could not be done in the web client that could be done in the desktop client. All of the series available in the desktop client are now available within the web client.

99% of the functionality of the Microsoft Dynamics GP desktop client is available in the web client; where a function is not available the menu option just won't be present in the web client. For example, the **Setup** section of the **Administration area page** in the web client (left side in the image, below) is missing several options such as **Process Server**, **Named Printers** and **Client Updates**.

Customizations created in **Dexterity** or **Visual Studio Tools for Microsoft Dynamics GP** will also work in the web client as they do in the desktop client; the customization method not supported in the web client are any done using **Modifier with VBA**. This is unfortunate as this type of customization was typically the easiest and quickest to do, but there appears to be no plan to bring them to the web client so any customizations using VBA will need to be rewritten using either Dexterity or Visual Studio Tools for Microsoft Dynamics GP.

Navigation Differences

The Microsoft Dynamics GP web client is similar in form and function to the desktop client, especially since the launch of Microsoft Dynamics GP 2013 R2 which saw the introduction of action panes to the desktop client.

However, there is a number of differences between the web and desktop clients in how you would navigate.

The first difference is the absence of a menu bar.

The **action pane** in the desktop client is not the same as that in the web client, with some entries such as *Options*, *File* and *Tools* being absent from the web client.

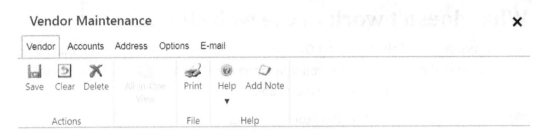

Another change is that the buttons at the bottom of many windows in the desktop client have, in the web client, become tabs on the action pane. For example, in **Vendor Maintenance** the buttons **Accounts**, **Address**, **Options** and **E-mail** at the bottom of the window have become tabs in the web client.

One of the key differences is the addition of ALT to the shortcut key combination. For example, in the desktop client *CTRL+L* can be used to open the Lookup windows, but in the web client this becomes *CTRL+ALT+L*. this is because *CTRL+[key]* shortcuts are taken by the web browser itself.

The biggest change to the web client, is that it is a single-window interface. This means you cannot have, say **Vendor Maintenance** and **Payables Transaction Entry** open at the same time.

You can still open **Vendor Maintenance** from within **Payables Transaction Entry** by clicking the **Vendor ID** field label, but it will overlay the transaction entry window when opened.

The final change to mention, is the addition of a **Search for Form or Report** window accessible from the search icon on the navigation pane:

As you start typing a window name, the forms and reports in Microsoft Dyna mics GP are searched and presented in the two sections of the window.

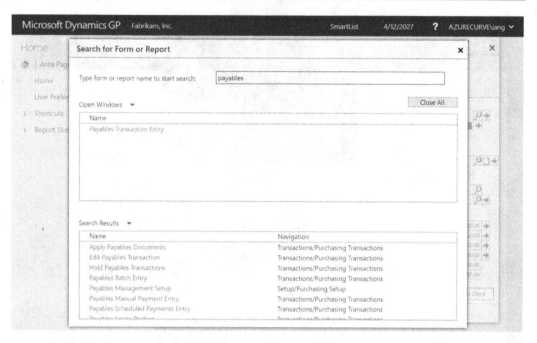

Any open windows matching the entered name is displayed in the top section and all other windows in the bottom section. Clicking the **Name** will open the window or report.

Integration with Microsoft Office

One of the key selling features of Microsoft Dynamics GP is the integration with the Microsoft stack; **SSRS** for reporting, **Exchange** and **Outlook** for email, **Word** for the **Word Templates** and **Excel** for exporting data. SSRS runs as a web client itself and the integration for integration with Exchange for email is still present.

The integration to Microsoft Office has been extended for the Word Templates. The original Word Templates were introduced in Microsoft Dynamics GP 2010 R2 as alternatives to the old Standard Reports with a small number of Word Template alternatives supplied by default.

Any Standard Report can be replaced with a Word Template just by selecting **Template** when printing the report and the Word Template version will be generated on the fly. This is a web client only feature which does not work in the desktop client.

Exports to Excel, such as from SmartList, work by generated the export for the standard browser functionality to download the file.

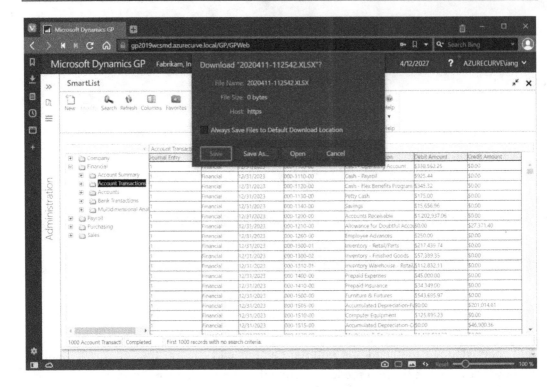

Web Client Administration

To complement the web client there is also a **web management console** which is used to administer the user logins. Access to the web client is via the address defined during the web client installation. To access the web client type the following into IE's address bar (change [server name] to the name of your server): https://[domainname]/ webmanagementconsole/ and then log in using a Windows domain account which is a member of the **Web Management Console Domain group**).

Once logged into the web management console click the **Session Manager** button at the bottom of the **navigation pane**. This will populate a list of session hosts in the top part of the navigation pane; clicking one of them will display details of current sessions on the selected session host in the area page to the right.

For each session on the session host, the created date of the session, the company being accessed, the GP User ID, GP version, Domain user ID, session id, tenant name and the last heartbeat (last activity by the session) are displayed.

If a session host is selected in the navigation pane the **Suspend** button in the ribbon can be pressed; this will prevent any other users being assigned to that session host.

When a session is selected in the list the **End Session** button on the ribbon will be enabled; clicking this button will then display a prompt asking for confirmation to end the session; confirm by clicking the **End Session** button:

As with the window in the desktop client, a session should only be ended if the session is really dead and the user is not processing anything in GP.

When a session is selected, as well as being able to end it, you can enable logging by clicking on the Logging button and then choosing whether to log Runtime, Script, Timing or SQL.

Summary

In this chapter we have logged into the web client, created a web client only user, taken a look at the navigation differences between the desktop and web clients, reviewed the integration with Microsoft Office and looked at how the Web Management Console can be used to manage the web client.

Index

Thank you for buying

Implementing the

Microsoft Dynamics GP

Web Client

Second Edition

Visit https://publishing.azurecurve.co.uk/ **for other titles from
azurecurve Publishing.**

www.ingramcontent.com/pod-product-compliance
Lightning Source LLC
Chambersburg PA
CBHW080603060326
40689CB00021B/4923